Dearest Audrey
I am so so
you have final
You're 70th — If you
not careful, you'll catch up! :)

Sunny Side Up

Love 'ya loads —
Lenore

Sunny Side Up

PRAYERS to BANISH the BLAHS and the BLUES

Bernadette McCarver Snyder

Published by Liguori Publications
Liguori, Missouri
http://www.liguori.org

Prayers in this book were adapted from an earlier book by Bernadette McCarver Snyder, titled *Everyday Prayers for Everyday People*, Our Sunday Visitor, 1984.

Library of Congress Cataloging-in-Publication Data

Snyder, Bernadette McCarver.
    Sunny side up : prayers to banish the blahs and the blues / Bernadette McCarver Snyder.
            p. cm.
        Rev. ed of: Everyday prayers for everyday people. 1984.
        ISBN 0-7648-0666-1
        1. Prayers. 2. Women—Prayer-books and devotions—English. I. Snyder, Bernadette McCarver. Everyday prayers for everyday people. II. Title.

BV283.W6 S67 2000
242'.8—dc21   00–041240

Printed in the United States of America
04 03 02 01 00   5 4 3 2 1

Contents

Part Three

Especially Now...

Part Four

As My Day Ends...

Part Five

I'm Grateful...

Introduction

ARE THERE DAYS when you want to pray but are too frazzled or too frustrated to find the words that you want to say? Maybe you just need a jump-start, a springboard to leap into a conversation with God.

I hope this little lighthearted book of prayers will help you jump for joy and leap forward when you feel like falling backward. It's my humble offering of prayers for different ages and stages, and lots of different everyday situations. Since every day IS different, maybe when you look through the Contents, you'll find just what you need for your "problem of the day." Maybe you will become my prayer partner—and then I think you will understand why I chose this dedication:

I dedicate this book
to my friends and family
who have often said of me,
"She hasn't got a prayer."

Part I

As My Day Begins...

And I Want Dawn Delayed

LORD, WHY DID You have to make the day start before my motor does? How can I look at sunnyside-up eggs at dawn when my sunny side won't be up for hours?

Wouldn't You like to rethink this early arrival of dawn, Lord, and make it come around noon so that I could have a long, leisurely sleep and then get up to have hot tamales or a hot fudge sundae for breakfast?

Yes, I know: I'm never satisfied. Here You created fabulous sunrises and threw in singing birds and fresh breezes—and I complain.

Truly, Lord, I am grateful for Your morning glories—but excuse me if I leave them for others to enjoy while I prop myself up with an elbow, sip hot black coffee, and stifle yawns. Forgive my early A.M. apathy, Lord. Just help me make it through the morning, and I promise to appreciate afternoon twice as much as anybody else.

I may miss the early bird, but I delight in the early-evening birdsong and cricket chatter. The morning school bus may be just a yellow blur to me, but I so enjoy the after-school play and chatter of children.

Dawn I will leave to the joggers and the alarm-clock makers—but I will exult in the warmth of the afternoon sun, the dusk filled

with fireflies, the moonlight, the star-shine, and the still of the night.

Thank You, Lord, for giving the world good things all day long: wonders for the late starters as well as the early risers. And one day, Lord, maybe You will wake me up with the early bird so I can actually see the dawn dawning.

But just one day, Lord—just one day.

And I See the Light

SLOWLY, SLOWLY, IT CAME, LORD. First the black turned into gray, and soon that melted into a lighter gray, and then palest violet crept in and subtly, softly it changed into shades of blue. And then the gold began.

Glittering splashes of gold, gentle yellows, and brilliant oranges poured over my world. Golden, golden morning had dawned.

Thank You, Lord, for today's sunrise. And for today's hope.

So often my life is like today's morning: black, Lord, so black. I am immersed in its blackness. And then, almost imperceptibly, You make it change. The black starts to turn to gray, and that's still bad, but not hopeless. And so I dare to start believing again and praying again.

And soon that lovely violet cheers me and fills me, and I reach out—and find tree branches full of the green leaves of hope silhouetted against the horizon of a blue sky. And then the mockingbird starts its morning calls. And the gold begins.

Thank You, Lord, for the golden dawn. Forgive me for ever doubting You in the darkness. Help me remember all the colors You have hidden in the blackness of the night. Give me the patience to wait for You to reveal them to me. Give me the courage to endure. Give me the love to understand.

And I Have the Blahs

HOW MANY TIMES I've seen a plant on a window sill, Lord, with its leaves drooping, its flowers folding—almost like it's pouting. Maybe somebody forgot to give it enough water or light. Maybe somebody just forgot to talk to it!

Actually, that's exactly the way I feel this morning, Lord. Like that plant, I'm drooping. I'm not sad or sick. I have no reason to be tired or troubled. I'm not even depressed or dejected. I've just got the blahs.

I guess I'm going to go dragging through the day, wanting to pout and not even knowing why. Maybe, like that plant, I need conversation. I need to talk to You, Lord.

I know I get busy, bustling about, scurrying in and out, hurrying and worrying about the tidbits of my life—and I forget the most important part: You. I don't take time to spend time with you in prayer. I don't talk to You—or sit still long enough to listen to see if You are trying to talk to me.

Forgive me, Lord. Help me remember how important it is to keep in touch. Perk me up today, so my leaves will stop drooping and the blahs will go away—and I can reach for the sun. Fill me and nourish me with Your goodness, and help me bloom where I've been planted.

And I Have Nothing to Wear

WHAT SHOULD I WEAR today, Lord? I know the lilies of the field don't worry about it, but I do. I am just not a natural-born lily. You are the one, Lord, who made me more of a ragweed than a rose—so You should understand why I spend more time trying to figure out what rags to put on to make myself feel like blossoming.

Every time I look into my closet, Lord, I have *nothing* to wear—even though the closet is full. Thank You, Lord, for giving me so many material possessions: wool material, cotton material, and the ever present polyester. Forgive me for complaining just because my wardrobe has few designer labels but lots of garage-sale tags.

The magazines all say that I can look just like this year's model simply by taking last year's shirt and some old slacks and "pulling it all together" with a new belt. Why is it that when I try something like that I look more pulled apart than pulled together?

I know, Lord. This is a ridiculous problem to be discussing with You when the world is facing wars and rumors of wars, hunger and pestilence, and the heartbreak of psoriasis. But You know I tell You *everything*, and this is my "problem of the day."

Thank You, Lord, for all the clothes in my closet. Forgive me for always wanting new ones. And help me, Lord, to "pull it all together"—both my wardrobe and my life.

And It's One Of Those Days

IT'S GOING TO BE ONE OF THOSE DAYS, LORD, I can tell.

Did You ever have one of those days, Lord, when You were working in the carpentry shop and You dropped the hammer on your toe, ruined a special piece of wood, or broke a tool just when You had to have a job finished by noon? Did a big storm come up and Your sandal strap come apart just when You were trying to make it to the next town before nightfall? Did the apostles ever promise to meet You and then show up late or start to squabble at the dinner table over something petty when You were trying to tell them something important?

I'm sure You know how I feel, Lord. You were here on earth, and here on earth it seems "one of those days" hits everybody at one time or another.

I know that I should be mature and well-adjusted enough to handle stress under fire—plus a daily portion of emergencies. But I don't want to think about that right now. I just want to sit down in the middle of the floor and feel sorry for myself.

So, Lord, touch me on the shoulder today and tell me it's going to be all right. Pat me on the head as You would a little child. Smile at me; bear with me; humor me."

And thank You, Lord, for giving me understanding, not only on "one of those days" but every day!

And I've Got Double Trouble

I'VE GOT TO QUIT leading this double life, Lord. It's wearing me out.

In the course of one day, I am expected to be a shrewd member of the work force, a down-home, understanding friend, an exciting and romantic spouse, and an expert at home decor, maintenance, management, and garbage disposal.

I feel double-crossed, double-timed, and double-whammyed!

I don't know how much longer I can go on this way, Lord. I'm developing a split personality.

Thank You, for filling my life with such variety—but teach me how to choose the right priorities, how to know what is important and when.

I know I shouldn't, but I feel as if I am supposed to be all things to all people, so there's seldom any time left for me. Help me to judge wisely, Lord, so I will manage to be wherever I am supposed to be whenever I am most needed. Help me to budget my time so there will be enough to go around for everyone, including me.

Give me double vision, Lord, so I can see the best way to handle my double life.

And I Learn to Fly

IT'S SO COMFORTABLE HERE, LORD—in my daily rut. It's so safe, sheltered, and familiar. As I look into the day ahead, I see so many unknowns, so many risks. I wish I didn't have to step out of my cozy little cocoon here.

Oh sure, Lord, I know that "same" may be boring—but it is so secure, so sure. I know I should be ready to evolve, to change, and to grow with whatever the day brings. I know I should climb out of my insecurities so that I can see the horizon that awaits me. I know that all of life is changing and that the end of change is death. Help me to accept—and maybe delight in—whatever changes come to surprise me today.

Remind me, Lord, of the caterpillar, destined to crawl along the ground—unless it undergoes the fearful chrysalis of change. Only then can it grow wings and soar heavenward.

Forgive my caterpillar comfortableness, Lord. Today, help me to open myself to new life and to trade in my rut of security for a chrysalis opportunity. Help me start to grow my wings so I, too—like the butterfly—can learn to fly, to soar, and to wing ever closer to You.

And I Have Sticky Fingers

IT'S NOT NICE to live life with sticky fingers, Lord. The models in the fashion magazines have lovely fingernails, beautifully painted with colorful polish. Why are mine always painted with strawberry jam?

While other people are starting the day with ambition, creativity, exercise class, or an emergency meeting at the White House, I am starting my day with sticky fingers. I am fixing toast with jam for everybody's breakfast, peanut butter and jam sandwiches for everybody's lunch bag, and trying to jam two hours of house-straightening into twenty minutes so I will have the rest of the day to go out and battle traffic jams. Somehow that doesn't sound as exciting as the White House.

Is this what it's all about Lord? Am I destined to spend my whole life in one kind of a jam or another?

Yes, Lord, I hear You. I know there are many hungry people who would be grateful to have strawberry jam. I even realize there are many people who wish they had a nice family like mine to give them sticky fingers. It's just that I have to complain to somebody, Lord, and You're the only one who listens when I talk.

So thank You, Lord, for the jam and my daily bread and the milk of human kindness and my sticky fingers. Forgive my com-

plaining and my ingratitude and my boredom. Fill me with your ingenuity and help me out of this rut.

Maybe I'll serve Eggs Benedict for breakfast tomorrow and put watercress sandwiches in the lunch bags. Maybe my fairy god-mother will send a limo to take me to work or to all the stops on my "to-do-today" list.

Or maybe I'll just learn to love sticky fingers.

Part II

It's Just Me, Lord...

Haggling

LORD, IS HAGGLING HABIT FORMING? I have been to so many garage sales that now when I am at a department store, I have this irresistible urge to say, "If I buy these two shirts will you throw in the yellow one for fifty cents?" At the grocery store, I have to bite my tongue to keep from blurting out, "I see the potatoes are sixty-nine cents a pound. Would you consider fifty-five cents a pound?"

That wouldn't be so bad, but I also find myself trying to drive a hard bargain with my family and friends. I'll say, "If you will do this or that, I will do that or this." And you know, what, Lord, I don't like that part of me. I don't like haggling my way through life, trying to keep the scales balanced so that I don't come out on the light side of convenience or opportunity or comfort.

I guess, Lord, that You must get pretty tired of my bargaining and haggling, since I've been dealing with You that way most of my life—even before I ever heard of garage sales. I know that I am always saying to You, "If you will just help me this one time, I promise I will never, ever again…." Well, You know what I am always telling You.

Forgive me for thinking I have to talk to You that way, Lord. Forgive me for thinking I have to haggle and make deals. Help me learn to put my life into Your hands, trusting in Your judgment, relying on Your mercy, truly believing that You know me better than I know myself and will wisely send me the way I should go, even though I may be convinced that it is the wrong path, the worst answer, and a terrible mistake.

Help me, Lord, to be like a leaf in the wind, freely going where You send me—without asking first, "Are You *sure*, Lord?" Help me be like the wildflower in the woods, blooming quietly and happily, without complaining about life being too dull or uneventful or risky, without watching out for my own best interests all the time, without shouting, "Look at me! Look at me!" Help me to stop trying to drive a hard bargain with my life and just go ahead and pay the price You ask.

But remember, Lord, I am only asking You to help me stop haggling about life—this does not apply to garage sales!

Trying to Shut My Mouth

LORD, IT'S TIME I FACED IT: I may as well admit that I have a speech disability. I can't stop talking.

I have reason to suspect that this is causing my family and friends traumatic tension, debilitating delirium, and perilous psychoses. In other words, I am driving them nuts.

The minute two or more are gathered together, I have the uncontrollable urge to spill the beans, spill the milk, and "share" my innermost thoughts, feelings, frustrations, and casual observations. When the phone rings, it is a call to action—and too often it is action of the jaw muscles no longer controlled by the brain muscle.

Now I know, Lord, that it is good to be open and able to communicate my concerns, but I think I have been overdoing it. Help me, Lord, to know when to shut my mouth and open my ears. Remind me to give my friends and family a break with equal time. Don't let me be so quick to pour out all my troubles before I look and listen to see if the other person is trying to get a word in edgewise, to tell me about a problem that needs some sympathy and time before it gets buried under the avalanche of my own recitation of the day.

Teach me, Lord, to bring my conversation to You first, so that

You and I together can decide how much of it is worth putting on the six o'clock news.

And bless my family and friends, Lord, for listening with love to my words without end. Amen.

Depressing Others

EVERYBODY AROUND HERE IS SICK of me, Lord. They think I'm depressing.

My great-aunt thinks I'm depressing because she gave me her favorite antique picture frame and I put a picture in it that she doesn't like.

My neighbor thinks I'm depressing because I'm always singing and happy when I'm working in the garden just when he's grumpy and grouchy because he has to cut the grass.

My friends think I'm depressing because I'm always discovering some new "unusual" restaurant or embarking on some new project and I expect them to get excited enough to discover and embark with me.

The credit card company thinks I'm depressing because I've called them four times about the error their computer has programmed into my bill and can't seem to program out.

But do You think I'm depressing, Lord? I keep coming to You with all my sad news and bad news—but I come to You with my glad news and good news, too. So at least we have a balanced relationship.

Thank You, Lord, for always listening and understanding—even when I'm depressing. Thank You for sympathizing with me and rejoicing with me.

And, Lord, I think You might be hearing from my great-aunt, my neighbor, and my friends—so I hope that won't depress You.

Being a Loser

THERE'S NO DOUBT about it, Lord: I am a loser. I am constantly losing my glasses, my pen, my car keys, my sense of humor.

I've been told, "You would lose your head if it wasn't tacked on." And you know, what, Lord? That's true! Even with my head tacked on, I have been known to lose it.

But the worst things to lose are those things I know I don't have to find right away. A friend wants to borrow a book and I go to get it but it isn't on the bookshelf where I was sure it would be. The temperature drops and I go to the closet to get my jacket but it isn't hanging where I was absolutely positive I left it. I suddenly have a need for something I carefully put away somewhere but I can't find where that somewhere is!

Even if the friend's in no hurry for the book and I can wear another jacket or do without the something I put away so carefully, I become compulsive about the "lost" being "found." I get so distracted I can't think about anything else! I'll search the house, every nook and cranny, even looking in ridiculous places. And if I don't find what I'm looking for, I'll go back and look in all the same ridiculous places again. In my frenzied search, I leave more important things undone and, even if I am able to resume my life temporarily, I'll continue to obsess about where the missing item might be.

It's not easy always being on the losing team, Lord. Help this born loser. Teach me to organize my shelves and my closets and my head. Then I can save all that time I waste looking for things and use it to look for You.

Remind me, Lord, that I may not be able to find a lot of things, but I will never really be a loser as long as I stay close to the One who said, "Seek and you will find." I *am* seeking, Lord. Draw me closer, guide me gently, and help me to keep looking until I find those pathways You want me to follow.

You are my Good Shepherd, Lord. Even when I stray into the wrong pasture, I know You will find me and bring me home. Thank You, Lord, for Your persistence.

But, Lord, if you know where that book or my jacket or any of that stuff is—*please* help me find them before I lose my patience, my temper, and my cool.

Hurting

IT HURTS, LORD. It hurts. I don't know how much longer I can handle this pain. It has become a grim presence that is always with me, a blanket that is smothering me, a fire that never burns out. I want to escape, Lord, to run away, to be free.

I look at other people who are pain-free and I am jealous. I want to be like them. I want to be alone again, without this constant companion of hurt and pain.

Remind me, Lord, that You, too, are my constant companion. Soothe me, sustain me. Remind me that You, too, have known pain. You suffered much more than I. Forgive my whining and give me courage. Hold my hand and give me strength. Console me. Comfort me.

The people I see every day, Lord, just don't understand. They don't know what it's like. Please tell them to be patient with me. I'm trying to overcome this, to think beyond the pain, to act like the person I was before this came into my life—but it isn't easy.

Please, Lord, if it's possible, help me find what I need to ease the pain and restore my health. But if it is not possible, help me to accept it—knowing that You will be with me to lead me beside the still waters. Although my cup does not seem to overflow these days, I will fear no evil—for I truly know You are with me.

Hurrying

THE HURRIEDER I GO, the behinder I get, Lord. I need help.

Help me to quiet down and listen up. Help me to pour out the stress and tension and hurry-up that fill me all the way to the lump in my throat. Replace the what ifs and wonder whys with Your blessed peace.

Help me learn how to plan, Lord, before the schedules overtake me and the deadlines drown me. Show me how to stop for just a few minutes each day to let Your gentle care wash over me and renew me.

Sometimes I wonder, Lord—is the hurry our cross? Is the worry our penance? If that's the way it is, then forgive me for complaining and show me how to conquer them before they conquer me. Help me learn to control my workload. Teach me to delegate, relegate, and expurgate. Show me how to stop the mutter and putter and get rid of the clutter. Give me the strength to do the work that matters, the gumption to relinquish the work that doesn't matter, and the wisdom to know the difference. Then Lord, maybe I can slow down, put my feet up, close my eyes, and listen for Your voice.

Running on Empty

I'M RUNNING ON EMPTY today, Lord.

I've used up all my energy, ideas, get-up-and-go, and stand-up-and-be-counted. All I have left is my sit-down-and-shut-up.

I've run around in circles so much that I've run out of steam.

What can I do, Lord, to get back my enthusiasm? How can I renew my vim and vigor so I can whistle while I work and let a smile be my umbrella?

When I am this tired, discouraged, and despondent, Lord, I need You to be my strength. Fill my emptiness with the enthusiasm of Your apostles, the courage of Your saints, and the joy of Your good news.

Bestir me with the beauty of Your creation; inspire me with the wonder of Your power; tickle my funny bone and touch my heart.

Whew! That sounds like a lot to ask, doesn't it, Lord? But when my battery is this low, it needs a really big jump start.

I am Yours, Lord. Although my feet are dragging and my spirit is flagging, I know you will prime my pump and fuel my tank. I know this, Lord, because whenever I have sent out a call for emergency road service before, You always answered my call.

Missing a Link

WELL, LORD, I broke my prayer chain again. There's a loose link here somewhere, and You and I both know it must be me.

Other people can keep their prayer links together—so why can't I? Other people seem to manage to set aside regular time to read Scripture, meditate, or participate in a Bible study group. They manage to say morning prayers, night prayers, polite prayers of please and thank You, and formal prayers they read from a book. Their chain is unbroken.

And then there's me, Lord—with my frantic schedule in which nothing I schedule ever seems to work out. If I plan to pray at 7 A.M. every day, for example, at 6:59 A.M. every day something unplanned will happen—the dog will choke on the newspaper he's dragging in, the oatmeal will overflow, the coffeepot will explode—and so will my plan. And when I tried joining a prayer-chain gang, they got my phone number wrong, so they never reached me to tell me who to pray for—and I soon became their missing link.

But, Lord, I know that You know that I do pray—in my own way—every day. Long ago I read somewhere that we should make our whole life a prayer by offering every thought, word, and deed to You. And so I give You my hurried, harried life, Lord. It isn't neatly packaged like formal prayers—in fact, it's kind of a mess. It isn't the same prayer in the same way at the same time every day—I can't predict or count on what may happen next. But it's truly Yours, Lord.

I want You to share it all—the good and the bad, the crazy and the serious. It isn't gift-wrapped all fancy with "amens" and "alleluias," but I hope you will accept it, Lord, with my humble love. And, Lord, I'm sorry about that broken prayer chain.

Wonder-ing

LORD, YOU KNOW how the philosophers are always discussing whether or not a tree falling in the forest makes a sound if no one is there to hear it? I really don't care much. But I *do* wonder if our neighborhood mockingbird's song would sound as sweet if I was not on the patio with my morning coffee to listen to it.

I wonder if the blossoms on the apple tree outside my bedroom window would look like a cloud of cotton candy if I wasn't there to notice.

I wonder if my son's tiny, chubby fingers would have been as exquisite if I had not been there to marvel at them and show them how to feel the softness of a flower petal, how to pet a puppy's ear, how to hold a spoon and wave good-bye and touch together to say a prayer.

I wonder if my husband is not really as handsome as I see him through prejudiced eyes. I wonder if my house is really not quite as dirty as I see it through guilty eyes.

I wonder if the evening sky is as awe-inspiring above those planets where there is no one to stand in the backyard and look up and feel finite against the infinite—as I do.

Thank You, Lord, for the morning birdsong and the evening symphony of stars, for the joy of springtime blossoms and the endless surprises you planted on this planet. Let the philosophers discuss while I delight in the wonders of Your world. But, Lord, about that crabgrass. Do You really think that was a good idea?

Learning to Listen

HAVE YOU NOTICED, LORD, how some children ramble on and on? A little kid will tell me about the dinosaurs and the dog and the kids next door. Another little kid will tell me a story about a giant bird that picked up a fat man and flew into the sky and dropped the man into a swimming pool and all the water flew out and knocked the lifeguard into a palm tree and a coconut fell down and…

Sometimes, after a while, I tune out the kids, the way I tune out television commercials. But sometimes, one of them may be trying to tell me something important just when I'm thinking about my chore list or the dentist appointment. That's when the kid has to tug on my sleeve or shout or maybe even get desperate enough to knock something off a table—just to get my attention. I should have been listening.

Forgive me, Lord. Help me learn to listen more carefully, to put aside my brain's "busy work" and pay attention. Remind me, Lord, that the kids—and the grownups, too—could get so tired of my tuning out that they give up and perhaps even stop trying to communicate with me.

And, Lord, while we're on this subject, You know that I ramble on and on, too, and sometimes, I wonder if You are about to tune me out. You wouldn't do that, would You, Lord? You *do* remember about that special intention I've been mentioning to You for the last six months, don't You? You *did* hear that, didn't You? Yes, I know You did. I know You hear all, know all, and love all. It's just that sometimes You seem to take an awful long time to answer. Forgive me for tugging at your sleeve so often. But that's the way children are, Lord. And I *am* Your child.

Feeling Overworked And Underpaid

I'M SICK OF IT, LORD. If I read one more article about a movie star who has just spent a million dollars building a swimming pool shaped like an artichoke, or a business tycoon who has just returned from his twenty-ninth trip around the world in his custom-made jet, or a lady who bought one lottery ticket (the first one she ever bought) and won two million dollars, I'm going to crawl into bed tonight and stay there indefinitely!

I work hard, Lord, and where has it gotten me? Tired. I try to do the best job I can. I am conscientious, loyal, dedicated—and I brush my teeth every day. But every time I take one step up the ladder, the ladder gets two steps higher. My raises never seem to equal my tax increases, and my careful budgeting never seems to cover expenses—much less leave room for jets or swimming pools or even lottery tickets.

What am I doing wrong, Lord? Why does my work load keep getting heavier and my paycheck lighter? Why am I overworked and underpaid?

Forgive me, Lord. Overlook my complaining and help me remember the millions of people who are unemployed and would be glad to have a job like mine and a paycheck like mine. But help me be realistic, too. Help me look objectively at my job and my paycheck and decide whether my salary is too little or my ego is too big.

If I am, in fact, overworked and underpaid, help me find a way to head in a new direction. And if I'm not, help me have a better attitude and learn to keep my mouth shut—except when I'm talking to You.

Living Life At Arm's Length

I'VE GOT TO BE CAREFUL TODAY, LORD. Recently, there have been a lot of people around here who will rush up and hug me when I least expect it. They are always talking about love and caring and sharing—and frankly, Lord, it embarrasses me. I don't mean to be critical—I mean, I know they are good people and I like being with them. But some days, I really want them to keep their distance.

Lord, I am not programmed to hug recklessly or to sit around talking about "feelings." It's hard for me to accept this new kind of love-life.

But then I think about You, Lord. I remember how the Bible tells about you sitting on the hillside with people, reaching out to them. I imagine You hugging your friends and followers and talking with them about loving one another, about caring for strangers, about sharing things in common so that everyone feels welcome.

Teach me, Lord. Help me to be comfortable with people who don't know how to stay at arm's length. Help me to accept fellowship and true Christian love—even when I feel it's too close for comfort. When I begin to live life at arms length, put Your arms around me and let me feel Your love so that I can pass it on. Remind me that arms were made for hugging, not for pushing away.

Making Choices

DECISIONS. DECISIONS. Will they never end? I order tea. Do I want it hot or cold? Do I want it with or without lemon? Do I want cream? Do I want sugar? I buy a house. Do I want wallpaper or paint? Do I want carpet or hardwood floors? Do I want this color or that color in the kitchen? I buy a car. Do I want an automatic or stick shift? Do I want custom wheels or regular? Do I want a CD player, extra speakers, a sunroof? Would I like a racing stripe?

And those are just the easy decisions, Lord. There are a lot of big ones, too. Should I move to another city or stay put? Should I try a new job or not? And that really big decision every day—what should I have for dinner? Oh, it never ends.

I worry and worry and finally make a decision. But as soon as I get one decision made, another pops up to boggle my mind and imagination.

Should I or shouldn't I? Can I or can't I? What if I do? What if I don't?

I'm tired of choosing, judging, determining, and settling, Lord. I don't want to be the judge or the jury or the determining factor any more. But I do want to settle—settle down in a nice, comfortable easy chair and let someone else make the decisions for me.

I'm sorry, Lord. I know I should be grateful that I have the power to decide. That's why You gave me free will, so I could share a little bit in Your power.

But the world's gotten so complicated, Lord. It just seems that

decisions never end—and I feel so unprepared, so ill-equipped, to decide wisely. Help me, Lord.

Sharpen my wits and heighten my intuition. Teach me to ponder sufficiently, decide wisely, and then forget it.

The forgetting is almost as hard as the deciding, Lord. It's so easy to keep going over and over things, wondering if I should have done something different after it's too late to change my mind. Don't let me do that, Lord. Don't let me spend my life bogged down in "what ifs."

Thank You, Lord, for the freedom to choose, even if it is hard.

But while we're on the subject, Lord, what do You think? Should I have chosen…oops, there I go again.

Listening to The Music of Life

AIR POLLUTION WAS BAD ENOUGH, LORD. I mean, who wants to live with smog and smoke and haze and bloodshot eyes. And water pollution is just terrible. Having cesspools instead of golden ponds is definitely not the way to add to the quality of life. But this *noise* pollution is the worst. My ears are getting worn out, Lord.

Today's society seems to think we must have music wherever we go. I watch a movie, and it has continuous music behind all the action. I go to dinner at a friend's house, and there's background music playing all night. I see joggers weaving in and out of traffic, and their ears are wired for sound. I see cars weaving in and out of joggers, and their radios are blaring music, carefully tuned to the highest decibel.

Yes, this noise pollution is definitely out of hand. But You know what the worst part is, Lord? There is so much noise that we actually have stopped hearing it. In self-defense, we have tuned it out. The most beautiful music may be playing in the background, but we don't really hear it until someone stops the conversation and calls our attention to it. Even news bulletins don't get through any more because we have heard too many of them.

We may be missing a lot of important things, Lord, because of this noise pollution.

Of course, for the same reason, we miss a lot of the important things You gave us. We've seen them so much that we don't notice them any more. Oh, sure, the spectacular sunsets and rainbows and autumn leaves grab our attention, but every day we pass by the robins and the caterpillars. We feel the sunshine and see the blue skies and move through the starry nights. But how often do their uniqueness or magnificence grab our attention? How often do we stop to enjoy and exult, to say thank You?

Forgive me for taking Your world for granted, Lord. Thank You for the wonders of Your creation. Help me to do what I can to respect Your creation and to take the time to smell the flowers along the way.

Help me to learn to tune out the unnecessary noise and still hear the music of life. Help me open my eyes and ears to the important things so I will always be tuned into the beauty and mystery of Your many-splendored universe.

Beginning Where I Am

LORD, IF I EVER WIN a sweepstakes, I just know that the dog will have eaten the ticket the day before. If I ever inherit a million dollars, I just know that I will have moved and left no forwarding address. If my ship ever comes in, I just know that I'll be waiting at the bus station instead of the dock.

Other people see opportunities as challenges and grab them and make something happen. I don't even notice the opportunities are there!

I don't just mean opportunities to make money or get ahead, Lord. There are so many other kinds of opportunities. For example, there are a lot of opportunities to do something good for others—people who need a smile or a compliment or a helping hand, if I would just notice them. I don't have to look to the other side of the world or even another state or city. There are plenty of opportunities right in my own neighborhood.

Help me to be more observant, Lord. Help me to see the chances to do Your work and spread Your word. Show me how to reach beyond my own little circle of self, how to recognize the needs and hungers of others, how to see others as You see them, Lord. Mother Teresa said, "Begin where you are." Help me to do that, Lord.

And the next time opportunity knocks, don't let me be away from home or in the shower. Let me hear the knock and come running to answer.

Needing Some Space

THE SPACE INVADERS have come, Lord. They're all around me. How can I escape?

I go out to take a nice little ride, and there's no space! It's been invaded by traffic—everywhere I turn.

I stop by to pick up a sandwich, and there is already a line of people waiting ahead of me. And soon, another line forms behind me.

I put aside some time to get a special job finished, and the doorbell rings. And then the phone rings—and rings and rings and rings.

Even when I get on an elevator—all alone—my space is invaded by piped-in music!

Forgive me, Lord. I *do* like people and music and even noise occasionally. But sometimes I need to find some peace and quiet. I long to go into the desert as You did, Lord—but there's no desert near my house.

You are my only hope, Lord. Help me to find just five minutes each day to spend with You—to let Your peace and joy wash over me and fill me. Then I will be renewed and refreshed.

And maybe when the space invaders come, instead of wanting to counterattack, I will be able to welcome them and take them to my Leader!

Longing for Yesterday

WHAT HAPPENED TO THE GOOD OL' DAYS, Lord, when life was simpler, people were friendlier, families were closer, skies were bluer, and never was heard a discouraging word?

I want to go back. I don't like the changes, the new ways, the modern inventions, the machines, the computers, the traffic, the hustle and bustle. Why do we have to have progress, Lord? Why can't things be like they used to be in those good ol' days?

Of course, we wouldn't have supermarkets full of delectable foods all year around—and we wouldn't have refrigerators or freezers in which to store all that great food. We wouldn't have television or airplanes or highways or modern hospitals or emergency numbers to call when we need help. And we wouldn't have electric coffeepots or carry-out fried chicken.

Maybe those good ol' days did need some improvement, Lord. Maybe, just maybe, *these* are the good ol' days after all.

Forgive me, Lord, for looking back. Although I thank You for the wonderful memories, don't let me dwell on them and miss out on today. Help me appreciate the present as much as the past. Help me see that You, Lord, are the source of all progress. Your world has been changing ever since You made it. It will continue to change, and I should adapt and appreciate it all.

With Your help I can do that, Lord, because I know that You have been, are, and always will be with me—past, present, and future. Your love is changeless.

Looking Ahead

HOW DID I END UP HERE, LORD? All these years I've been antic- ipating the future—studying for the future, planning for the fu- ture, looking forward to the future. Then, suddenly I find myself here, today, realizing that I'm there. This *is* the future.

I've reached the middle. I passed "go" and did not collect $200. Now what am I going to do, Lord? How can I look forward to the future when I'm already in it?

How did this happen so fast? Where did the past go, Lord? What did I do with it all? I know. I spent it studying, working, reaching for the next rung on the ladder, trying to become an adult, trying to accomplish things I thought were worthwhile. But the future became the present, and I didn't even realize it or cel- ebrate it or have a parade or rent a billboard. I didn't notice the past turning into the present or the present making way for the future—and here it is.

Of course, You planned it that way, didn't You, Lord? You ar- ranged it so that our todays become memorable yesterdays and our tomorrows turn into fulfilled todays. And still there's more to come—an endless supply of tomorrows, not just in this life but in the next as well! Who says you can't eat your cake and have it, too?

Thank You, Lord, for letting me live in the future—and still have a future to anticipate.

Enjoying the Ride

WELL, LORD, I'M ON MY WAY AGAIN. Why is it that I am always on my way yet never seem to get anywhere?

I am always on my way to a better job, a bigger salary, a new hobby, a new house, a new personality, a better body, a healthier frame of mind, a deeper prayer life. I am quick to start but slow to arrive.

What's wrong with me, Lord? Am I destined to always be hitting red lights or stopping to ask directions? Do I take too many detours or run out of gas too fast?

Help me, Lord, to learn how to read the road signs better. Help me to be a little more careful in making my travel plans. Be my tour guide.

But, Lord, maybe I'm just one of those people who never really "arrives." If I am, that's all right. The scenery is wonderful along the way, and the turns in the road are full of surprises. Don't let me miss any of it, Lord. Teach me how to enjoy the trip.

Being Afraid Of the Dark

I'M SCARED, LORD. I'm afraid of the dark at the top of the stairs and at the bottom of the stairs, out the back door and around the corner. Most of all, Lord, I'm afraid of the dark in today's world.

Everywhere I look today, Lord, the dark side seems to show up. There's darkness in entertainment, politics, businesses, schools, the legal system—even homes. It's scary, Lord.

I used to be able to go to the movies or watch TV with my family or friends and look forward to having a good time. Now I have to be so careful; no matter how cautious I am about choosing entertainment, there's still the risk that something dark will be lurking there. I used to be able to admire our leaders, heroes, stars—the people who had made it to the top. Now I find myself being suspicious of them. And the family—the *home*—used to be something I could always count on, but now the spreading darkness seems to have seeped in to cast shadows there, too.

Light a candle, Lord. Show me where to step in the darkness. I know Your light is still bright in the world, and I just have to find it and follow it. Give me the courage to keep looking for it. I know it won't be too bad if I'm afraid of the dark as long as I never get afraid of the Light.

Lead me to Your Light, Lord, so I can follow You home.

Holding On

EVEN WHEN I'M JUST BARELY HOLDING on by my fingertips, Lord, I just can't let go. Once I have latched onto something, I just can't make myself unlatch.

I take on a committee job, and after I've worked on it too much and too long and I know I should let it go, I keep struggling with it just a little longer, reluctant to let someone else take over "my" job. I accumulate stuff in my basement and I know I should clean it out and get rid of it, but I keep putting it off, telling myself I just might need some of it, knowing I won't but hesitant to even let go of junk!

When someone is leaving, I drag out the good-byes, thinking of last-minute things to say. When the autumn leaves are already falling, I put off putting away the things of summer, hoping for just a few more warm, sunny days.

It's no wonder I find it so hard to let go of my children—knowing that they are old enough to have independence, but afraid to let go.

Forgive my insecurity, Lord. Give me the courage and confidence to "hold tight with open hands."

Teach me how to open my heart as well as my hands. Help me to empty myself so that I can be filled with Your will and Your peace. Help me to give in, to give up—but only to You. Help me to really know what it means to "let go and let God."

Hoping For Something Lasting

LORD, DO YOU KNOW WHAT it's like to live in a "throwaway" society? Nothing ever gets fixed or saved anymore because everything is geared to obsolescence. As soon as anything breaks down or gets frayed around the edges, we just toss it aside. Where will it all end, Lord? Are we beginning to treat people that way as well?

My grandmother told me that children a few generations ago would treasure the one toy they got for Christmas, taking care of it and saving it for years. Some of them still had those toys when their own children were growing up. People back then had only a few books and would pass them lovingly from hand to hand. They had one set of cloth napkins, which were washed and ironed over and over again for hundreds—or maybe thousands—of family meals. They didn't have many material possessions, but everything they had was carefully preserved to be reused or recycled or handed down.

It's not like that anymore, Lord. Today's children have rooms full of toys, most of which don't last long enough to get saved or treasured. There are a lot of books around, but few people really value them as treasures to be saved for future generations. And those cloth napkins have turned into paper that can be thrown out at the end of the meal—without a second thought. Yes, we have a lot of material possessions now, Lord, but too few of them are preserved or recycled or handed down.

All our "make do" has turned into "pitch out," Lord. Even our friendships are geared to obsolescence. Today everybody is always on the move—changing jobs, changing neighborhoods, changing interests—so friendships are often temporary, fleeting, and subject to change without notice.

I'm tired of this throwaway society, Lord—tired of adjusting to today's shifting sands, tired of wondering what or who is going to be pitched out next. Give me something to hang on to, Lord, some security, some assurance, something lasting.

Forgive me, Lord, for being part of the problem—for being too careless with material possessions, for too often tossing out instead of making do, for sometimes treating people the same way, giving up on friends and relatives instead of trying to preserve and save the relationship we share.

Teach me, Lord, to appreciate what I have and to hold on to it. Remind me that You are my security and my assurance in this changing world. Stay with me so I won't get thrown by my throwaway society.

Getting on the Scale

LORD, EVERY MAGAZINE article I read tells me to "widen my horizons," to "broaden my viewpoint," and to "expand my sensibilities." I don't think it's working right, Lord. The only thing this sitting and reading articles has accomplished is to widen my middle, broaden my rear view, expand my dress size—and destroy my self-image.

I imagine myself thin and glamorous, taking my viewpoint and sensibilities and heading for a new horizon. Then I look in the mirror and realize I am overweight and under suspicion. Anyone who takes a second look at me must view me suspiciously, wondering if I am in training for the Overeaters' Olympics, conducting a scientific research project on how to dine like a gluttonous Roman emperor.

Lord, help me learn to love spinach more than Southern fried chicken. Make me take second helpings of celery instead of cheesecake. Show me that cottage cheese has more inner beauty than chocolate (and leads faster to outer beauty.)

Thank You, Lord, for all the beautiful foods You have given us, the bounty of your land, the yield of your harvests—and help me to love them less.

Shrinking Faster Than a Violet

WHY AM I SHY, LORD—why? Shrinking violets in the shady forest may be lovely, but in the rest of the world, it's another story. Today everyone is climbing the ladder, reaching for a rainbow, looking up. Except the meek—who still have not inherited the earth.

In the forest, some plants keep growing higher and higher, reaching for the sun. But the quiet little plants on the forest floor just *adapt* until they can get by with less light and less sunshine in their life. Is that what I've done, Lord?

Have I adapted instead of growing? Have I let my shyness hold me in place like a spider's web? Or am I being too self-conscious? Should I just accept what I am and stop asking why?

Help me, Lord, to know when to stay quiet and when to speak up. Help me to know the difference between being shy and being insecure and afraid. Or is there a difference? Sometimes I think people wonder if I am just naturally quiet or just naturally have nothing to say!

Help me, Lord, to overcome enough of my shyness to be what You want me to be. And if You want me to stay shy, help me learn to live happily without any of the limelight, and maybe even with a little less sunshine. You will be my light, Lord, because I know You love the shrinking violet as much as the mighty oak.

Feeling Locked Out Again

LORD, HAVE YOU EVER SEEN a grown man, wearing a short-sleeved shirt, standing in the snow on a patio, peering through a glass sliding door, begging a two-year-old child to "please unlock the door so Daddy can come in"? If You have, Lord, that man was my husband.

Today, in the July heat, I was just remembering that cold December day when I left for the grocery store and my husband came out to remind me to bring home his favorite snack. In the few seconds it took him to walk back to the kitchen door after I had driven away, our two-year-old son had closed the door, and it had automatically locked.

Through the closed door, my husband tried to explain to our toddler how to turn the lock. But after a while the garage began to get awfully cold, and he could hear the whimpering beginning when our son started getting worried about Daddy not coming back in the door. So his next move was to trudge through the snow around to the back yard up to the glass patio door.

Naturally, it was locked, too. But now our son was delighted because he could *see* Daddy, and he started giggling at how funny Daddy looked out there in the snow, making gestures through the door.

Finally, my husband managed to get the kid to turn the latch on the patio door, and by the time I got home, the boy was tucked snugly in bed and the daddy was tucked snugly on the sofa with two blankets around him, his feet in a pan of hot water, and a hot drink in his hand.

The more I think about that, Lord, the more it reminds me of the way Your people treat You sometimes. In an unguarded moment, we close the door and it automatically locks.

Then You keep trying to get our attention, and we fumble around with the lock on the door, whimpering because we can't understand Your directions and we aren't smart enough to make it open by ourselves. Sometimes we laugh when we see You on the outside while we are on the inside, not realizing that we need You inside with us if we are to be safe and secure.

Forgive our childishness, Lord. Help us to keep the door open for You always, so we will never be alone and we will have You with us to hold our hand and tuck us in at the end of a long day.

Part III

*Especially
Now...*

When I'm Stuck In Traffic

WELL, HERE I AM AGAIN, LORD—stuck. This is called an *expressway*, but it's more like a truck stop—a truck in front of me, a truck on each side of me—and none of us moving. We're in a fifty-five-mile-per-hour zone, but we're traveling at a fifty-five-mile-per-week speed.

Who are all these people on this road anyway, Lord? Where are they going? Why are they going? And when are they going to get going and get out of my way?

It's like this all the time: hurry up and wait. Speed up, slow down—and stop.

All these people in cars and trucks may be the same people I hurry up and wait with every day. I don't know. We never look at one another. That isn't part of the game plan.

These people may have some of the same problems and worries and fears that I have, but I'll never know that, Lord, because I'll never know them as real human beings. I see them simply as obstacles in my way.

The game plan calls for us to switch lanes and cut in front of one another, to travel in the fast lane if we can. As soon as we see a driver in a "faulty" car—old or dented or defective—slowing down, we are supposed to pass by quickly and leave that driver to eat our dust.

Is that what my life has become, Lord? Do I act that way on the other roads I travel as well?

Forgive me, Lord. Help me to slow down, to really look at my fellow travelers in life. Help me to see them as real people who are as frustrated as I am. Help me to care and to let others know I care.

Every day, Lord, I become a citizen in a city of cars—but I don't know any of my neighbors. Please don't let that happen in the rest of my life, Lord. When I get too smug and stuffy, nudge me to roll down my window and let some fresh air blow in. When I start to exceed the speed limit, help me put on the brakes. And remind me, Lord, not to blow my own horn so often.

But, Lord, I'm really in a hurry right now—so could You please make that truck in front of me hurry up and get out of my way?

When I'm Judging By Appearances

LAST NIGHT, I WENT TO an exotic restaurant to have a new "dining experience." When the food came, everything on my plate was dark green, brown, or beige. I didn't even want to think about putting that food into my mouth, but I forced down my gag reflex and screwed up my courage and took a bite. The food was delicious! Once again, I had judged by appearances.

Some days, Lord, I judge my life that way, too. I look at what has been put on my plate, and I see only dark green, brown, or beige. No excitement, no oranges, no reds, no purples—just the same dull routine: do what I have to do, run here, run there, meet my responsibilities. That gag reflex kicks in, and I don't want to pick up my fork.

Forgive me, Lord. I know routine is necessary and, once I dig into it, it's not so bad after all. In fact, I almost always find bright splashes here and there—shared laughter with a friend, a bit of surprise good news, a happy phone call, an invitation to a pizza party.

So, Lord, help me remember how delicious life can be even when it looks boring. Help me see beyond the ordinariness and taste the spice of Your love and creativity. Help me find a new hobby, interest, or direction, so that life will look more colorful. Show me how to step out of my ordinariness by reaching out to help someone else. Show me how to make the most of my ordinariness by learning how to do the ordinary things I do extraordinarily well.

And thank You, Lord, for the dark greens and browns and beiges. Without them, we wouldn't realize how bright and wonderful it is when You send along a splash of pink or a glint of gold, or suddenly paint a whole shining rainbow in a sky that seemed completely gray.

When I'm Nearing Burnout

COMPUTERIZED, AUTHORIZED—electrically, electronically, efficiently depersonalized. That's what this world is beginning to seem like to me, Lord. Machines, machines, everywhere—and not a shoulder to cry on.

I'm tired, Lord—tired of the hustle and bustle, the putdowns, the one-upmanship, the need to stay on your toes, ahead of the pack, out front, at the top of the heap. I don't want to take any more self-improvement courses, read any more self-fulfillment books, watch any more motivational films, or become best friends with another new computer.

Instead of dancing to the tune of the alarm clock every morning, I want to dance to a different tune. Instead of hurrying into the day's work, I want to slow down and take a stroll through the park. And I want to trade in my get-up-and-go for a nap in the afternoon.

Yes, Lord, I have all the symptoms of burnout, overload, and terminal tiredness. Help, Lord—before I also get complainer's complaint!

Lord, maybe I need to look at my life and my work and decide whether my burnout symptoms mean I should quit my job or just quit trying to keep up with all those machines. Those time-saving, work-saving machines have their jobs to do and I have mine.

Those machines represent progress—but I represent You. Those machines can't smile or sympathize or understand or lend an encouraging word—but I can. Those machines weren't made in Your image, Lord—but I was. And I thank You.

When I'm Sick

I'M SICK, LORD; I need some sympathy. I need someone to hold my hand and soothe my brow and bring me homemade chicken soup.

I'm tired of feeling sick and staying in bed, and trying to act brave and take my medicine and wait. I want to be well *now*, Lord, *now!*

Yes, I know, Lord. I should be a patient patient. I may be sick, but I don't have to be sickening! I should trust in You and hope in You. But it's so hard. Help my doctor find the right medicine, Lord, and help me to take my medicine with courage and hope.

Help me understand that Your way is always the best way but not always the easy way. Teach me to follow, even when the road leads uphill. As I stumble along in the dark, help me remember that You can see through the shadows to the warmth of light even though I cannot.

Hold my hand, Lord. Lead and I will follow.

When I'm Depressed

I'M LOOKING OUT MY WINDOW this morning, and everything looks gray and depressing. Oh, I know the trees are lush green, full of promise and freshness—but to me, they look shadowy, even threatening, like sentinels outside a prison cell.

Sometimes I feel like a prisoner—trapped. I'm tired of staying in, but I feel too sad and empty to try to go out.

I see the flowers in the garden awash with color, smug and satisfied with their beauty. How dare they be so bold and bright, always showing off, calling attention to themselves. I could never do that. But then, of course, I don't feel beautiful. I don't want anyone to look at me for fear they'll see the terror and anger in my eyes.

I see birds soaring and swooping, looking down on me here below, earthbound—and they keep right on singing. What do they have to sing about? They don't know where their next meal is coming from. At least I know that much. I can't fly and I don't feel like singing, but at least I have a roof over my head and food for the day—and even the week.

What's the matter with me, Lord? Why do I let myself get depressed when I know I have so much to be thankful for? Please take away this awful gray blanket of gloom that keeps falling over me. I can't do it alone, Lord. I've tried, but I can't. I need You—Your strength, Your joy, Your optimism.

Please, Lord, give me back the eyes that once could see all the beauty around me. Give me back the music, the sparkle, the spice.

I'm tired of being depressed, Lord, and cold and dull and bored. I want to see the color again, and to feel. Oh, Lord, I want to feel again. I want to giggle and discover and expect.

And I know I can, Lord, with Your help. In fact, I think I feel better already. Just talking to You and saying it all out loud has made me see how silly I am. I'm going to do something right now. I'm going to stop feeling sorry for myself and start feeling something else—anything else.

Of course, I know my resolve is weak. I may be right back, crying again, tomorrow. But I promise You, Lord, I *will* come back to You. I'll bring You my depression and offer it up and let You help me make something different out of my life. I promise You I won't sit looking out this window anymore, waiting for the world to come to me, waiting for someone else to cheer me up. With Your help, Lord, I can cheer myself up. I can find something that will help me feel better—something to do or wear or eat or start or read or study or listen to or like.

I'm going to feel more beautiful than the flowers, and the birds will be jealous of my song. Look out, world, here I come.

When I Live With Small Children

LORD, I KNOW FROGS are fascinating. I know peanut butter is nutritious, and not just the superglue that sticks together pages of recipe books and small ponytails and blue-jean pockets. I know the endless whir of those plastic Big Wheels™ racing up and down the driveway means that healthy little legs are peddling them.

I know that jelly fingerprints and muddy footprints and dirty diapers and dirty looks and little noses to be wiped and skinned knees to be bandaged are not major crises, that they can be handled with a bit of patience and love.

But, Lord, how I long for a whole day with grownups—a whole day when I don't have to think about or talk about potty training or sandboxes or sibling rivalry, a day when I can be a real person again, an individual, instead of a nose wiper or games director.

Lord, remind me of how lucky I am to have this special time of life—an opportunity to see the world fresh and new through the eyes of a child, to discover and delight in all the wonders that only a child can see. Remind me, Lord, that this time will never come again. I will never be able to come back to these days, to take a little hand in mine, to sit on the grass, to giggle together or watch a butterfly or be enchanted by a leaf or a colored rock or a snowflake.

Thank You, Lord, for this special, never-to-come-again time of my life. Don't let me mess it up by spending my hours complaining and correcting instead of teaching and sharing. Don't let me lose today by always waiting and hoping for tomorrow.

But, Lord, could You see Your way clear to let me have next Tuesday off?

When I Live With Teenagers

LORD, WHEN YOU LIVE with a teenager, you feel like you're living in a parenthesis!

Somewhere back there is your "past life"—the time when you were in control, when you were the authority figure, the expert, the one who had all the answers, the one in charge. And somewhere ahead is your "afterlife"—after the teen becomes an adult and hopefully will no longer be a self-appointed expert on every subject, will no longer need an extra ten dollars every thirty minutes or consider dirty tennis shoes an appropriate centerpiece for the kitchen table or consider you a totally uninformed tyrant who is trying to ruin everything with your stupid house rules.

In the meantime, Lord, here I am caught in the middle, in this parenthesis time. Help me, Lord, to maintain my dignity in spite of constant attacks on my self-esteem, to hold on to my values and principles while constantly being told they are old-fashioned, to keep my chin up even though my mouth is always falling open at the latest teen pronouncement or escapade!

Help me, Lord, to see the promise and possibilities of these special years. Help me to step back and "see" with teen eyes, "hear" with teen ears (even if it means a high-decibel attack on my eardrums), "feel" with teen psyches, "hurt" with teen sensibilities.

Help me to remember how frightening it can be when life is just beginning to bud and the blossom is still only a promise, the future only a dream. Help me to remember how exciting it can be to "discover" philosophy, science, ancient Egypt, or a new idea that will surely save or change the world. Help me to remember how much it hurts when an adult squelches your enthusiasm or questions your ability or doubts your maturity.

Help me to use this parenthesis time, Lord, to draw my teens safely within the parenthesis of my protecting arms, to give them the assurance that they are liked even when I question, and loved even when I discipline.

Thank You for the past time, Lord—the bedtime stories, the Halloween nights, the Christmas mornings, the hugs and kisses and whispered secrets. Help me live today wisely, Lord, so that I can also look forward to a happy "after" time when my teens-turned-adult will still be on speaking terms with me and might even remember me as a friendly tyrant or a "fun" dictator.

To make sure of that, Lord, please help me now to give understanding as well as advice, praise as well as criticism. Help me to share this exciting time without intruding or antagonizing my teens. Help me to walk that fine line between tyranny and indulgence. And remind me, Lord, to be objective enough to laugh once in a while so that I can make the most of these years of living a parenthesis.

When I Live With Senior Citizens

LORD, WHY DO PEOPLE have to wear out? When the car or refrigerator starts acting funny, we can get if fixed or trade it in. But human beings aren't so lucky. When one of our parts quits working right, we usually have to go on living with it.

It's so hard, Lord, to see those we love start wearing out, to see them get forgetful or lame, their eyes or ears failing and joints stiffening. I know I should be understanding and patient, but it's hard to live with, day after day.

Remind me, Lord, that it is probably even harder for them. I try to be sympathetic, but soon the sympathy turns toward myself. I keep thinking how awful it is that *I* have to put up with the aggravation and irritation. I forget that *they* are putting up with the pain and disability. Forgive me, Lord. Help me.

I think the most difficult part is the acceptance. I don't want to see them weak or dependent. I expect my elders to be strong and protective of *me*, just as they were when I was a child. I don't want to accept the fact that they are wearing out, because that means I have to grow up. I have to assume the responsibility, take over the burden, and be the strong and protective one. I don't like that, Lord.

I have enough trouble taking care of the younger generation, and now I have to take care of the older generation as well. When is it going to be my turn to take care of *me*?

Lord, I know this sounds like sniveling, like I'm shirking my duty—and that worries me. I want to be brave and wise and sympathetic and understanding; I want to be a saint. Instead, I find myself gritting my teeth and almost feeling hatred for a person I used to love so much.

I can't say this to anyone else, Lord. I can't even say it out loud to myself. That's why I have to talk to You about it.

I don't like old age. I don't like senility. I don't like the idea of a useful, vibrant person becoming childish again, dependent and useless, with parts that don't work right anymore and can't be replaced. Why do You let it happen, Lord, why?

Yes, I hear You, Lord. There are many things I cannot understand but accept on faith. And now that I've said it all to You, maybe I will feel better and can go on—for another hour or another day. Maybe with Your help I can learn to accept if not understand, to endure if not excel.

I know now that I can't be a saint and handle it perfectly, but maybe I can at least handle it with good grace. Show me how, Lord. Stand with me. Help me to be stern and demanding when it is necessary but soft and loving when it is needed. Help me to stop gritting my teeth when I see the weakness and childishness. Remind me that there may have been a double meaning when you said, "Suffer the little children to come to me."

When I Need To Calm Down

"BE SURE BRAIN IS ENGAGED before putting mouth in gear!"

I would like to think, Lord, that a motto like that would help cure my "open-mouth syndrome"—but so far it has been as successful as the voyage of the *Titanic*. Each time I decide to forcefully drive home a point to someone, I neglect to turn on the brain first and I strip my gears.

As my voice gets louder and louder, my brain tries to send a message through to my voice box to tell it that the calm, rational approach works much better than the hysterical approach. But since I did not engage the brain before putting mouth in gear, the message never gets through.

I can hear myself saying all the wrong things but I can't seem to stop my runaway mouth. What can I do, Lord?

Some people learn from their mistakes. Some even earn from their mistakes. Oh, to be one of the learners or earners instead of one of the habitual mistakers!

Couldn't You help me, Lord? The next time I start harassing and haranguing, couldn't You part the earth beneath my feet and just let me fall through? Or at least override my control box and turn on my brain for me?

Help me, Lord, to make my voice gentle, my instructions loving, and my message understandable. Whenever my voice level and my blood pressure start rising, remind me of that famous saying, "Make your words tender today—for tomorrow you may have to eat them."

When It's Not My Fault

IT'S NOT MY FAULT, LORD. I didn't mean to be late. How did I know the dishwasher was going to overflow and pour buckets of bubbles all over the kitchen just when I was ready to leave? I didn't know that would happen just because I put in the wrong detergent.

It's not my fault, Lord. I didn't mean to put a dent in the fender. How could I guess that somebody would have parked right behind me at an angle instead of in the marked parking spaces? I looked both ways to see if anything was coming. I just didn't think to look behind me to see if something had already come and stayed.

It's not my fault, Lord. I didn't mean to forget to put the salt in the picnic basket. I know tomatoes and hard-boiled eggs taste awful without it. I can't help it if I overlooked it just because I was in a hurry, just because I took time to wash my hair, sweep the patio and call Jane about the luncheon before I realized it was time to leave and I hadn't packed the basket yet.

Lord, Lord, why am I always spouting forth alibis for myself? Every time a new disaster occurs, I feel so guilty. I always want things to be just perfect, but often I goof up. And then I have to have an alibi, an excuse, a reason—something so I can forgive myself.

Excuse me, Lord. You and I both know I make mistakes, and You and I both know I don't mean to. It's just that I'm sometimes scatterbrained, disorganized, or optimistic. Did I say "sometimes"? You and I both know better than that, too.

I am always so optimistic I think I can get fourteen things done in fifteen minutes. I think I can make two stops on the way to a given destination and still get there on time even though I only have five minutes to make it when I leave home. I believe I can leap tall buildings in a single bound and wrap up big jobs in little time and tie together loose strings in no time at all!

Let's face it, Lord. I am not superhuman and I may as well realize it. Thank You for making me optimistic, Lord—but I think it's time for You to make me a little realistic, too. No, I guess I have to make myself that. But I'll need Your help, Lord—as usual.

Help me learn to mix my optimism with organization, my penchant for perfectionism with practicality, and my scatterbrained style with a better scheduling system! Make me stop underestimating the time required to do a job and overextending my limited capabilities.

But, Lord, if I still sometimes goof up, remember—it's not my fault!

When I'm In The Hospital

I'M TOO SICK to be in this hospital, Lord. Don't these people realize that I feel too bad to keep sticking my arms out to get stuck with needles, to keep taking sponge baths, eating food I don't like, and smiling cheerfully at nurses, doctors, volunteers, and assorted visitors (whom I love to see coming but also love to see going because I'm too sick to keep smiling)?

And why is everything so white and cold, steely and sterile? I guess the medical world thinks this looks professional and inspires confidence. Instead, it just inspires fear.

I keep thinking about how expensive all this equipment looks, and how impersonal and mechanical everything is, as though it were never meant to be used on real-life people like me.

And, Lord, when I'm afraid of the machines and the expense and the feeling that I'm in a twilight zone, I get nervous and cranky and suspicious. Then if someone makes a mistake in this unreal, removed environment—even a little mistake like bringing me milk for lunch instead of the juice I ordered or forgetting to bring the extra blanket they promised—it looms larger than it would in the "real" world. I start wondering if they might make a mistake on my medicine or my orders for bed rest or any of a million things I begin to imagine.

Lord, help me to stop wasting my energy worrying about what

could happen when I should be saving all my energy to try to cure what has already happened. I know there are people all over the world who are sicker than I am, and many are lying in a gutter or an alleyway or in a mud hut or a drafty shack, while I am in a clean, antiseptic room with hardworking professionals taking care of me. Forgive my irritation, Lord, my lack of trust in You as well as in Your people.

Ease my nerves, relax my muscles. Help me to accept the pain and discomfort and to stop complaining and criticizing. Help me to remember how many have suffered more than I have. Give me the courage to face whatever today brings, and the faith to anticipate a better tomorrow.

And thank You, Lord, for letting me be in a hospital as nice as this one—even though I'm too sick to be here!

When Someone I Love Is in the Hospital

THE WAITING IS THE HARDEST PART, LORD; the waiting and the wondering. I wonder how the tests will come out and when the lab report will come back. I sit in the surgery waiting room for two hours, getting more scared every second because the doctor told me the operation would take only thirty minutes. I wonder when someone will come to talk to me and what the news will be when he or she does come.

It's hard, Lord, to just sit and wait when I'm used to working and doing.

And why is it so quiet and so carpeted, Lord, so unlike real life? I feel that I should whisper and tiptoe all the time, and soon it seems as if I am in one of those eerie movies and something ominous is bound to happen in this hushed, almost hostile environment.

I know, Lord, the peace and quiet must be good for the patients, but it's hard on the nerves of the watchers and waiters.

I want to do something, but there's nothing to do. I want to help, but no one will let me. I want to make this pain go away, but I know I can't.

And I feel so guilty, Lord. I'm not the one who is hurting or sick, and yet it's so easy to get restless and feel put-upon. My life has turned topsy-turvy, and I have to keep changing appointments and rearranging my usual routine so I can find time to spend at the hospital. I race through traffic to get here, but once I'm here, there's nothing to do but wait.

Forgive me, Lord. Help me to use this quiet time for prayer instead of panic. Watch and wait with me, Lord. Help me listen for the nurses' footsteps. Help me watch the doctor's expression for clues of the truth.

Be with me, Lord, so I can turn the wondering toward the wonder of Your friendship and fill the waiting time with Your timeless mercy and love.

When I'm Grouchy

LORD, I CAN'T STAND THOSE PEOPLE who are forever saying things like "Happiness is a warm smile," "Smile and the world smiles with you," "A frown is just a smile turned upside down." That's easy for them to say!

What do they know about my life and its frown factor? What do they know about irritations and aggravations?

It's easy to be cheerful if things are going good—or if I'm just too stupid to understand that they're actually going bad. Maybe those people who are always pasting smile faces on things just don't understand the situation!

No, Lord, I guess I'm the one who doesn't understand the situation. I get in a bad mood and the whole world looks like a smile turned upside down. I know I should try to be more cheerful and realize that I'm not the only one with problems. In fact, there are probably many with problems much worse than mine, and they manage to keep smiling.

Forgive my grouchiness, Lord. Help me wipe the frown off my face and be more tolerant of the sunshine peddlers.

But, Lord, don't expect me to be drawing smiley faces on notes today. I'm just not in the mood for that much cheer. And forgive me, Lord, if I lapse into an occasional scowl. How else will my eyebrows ever get any exercise?

When My Body Doesn't Know What's Good for It

THERE'S SOMETHING WRONG with my body, Lord. It doesn't know what's good for it!

At times, I crave terrible things like doughnuts and hot fudge sundaes and chili on top of hot dogs with onions and cheese. I never crave anything like squash or rutabagas or unflavored yogurt.

When I decide to improve my diet and my health, I start by having cereal with fiber for breakfast, fresh green salads with low-cal dressing for lunch, and dinners that consist of just a tiny bit of meat with a lot of vegetables—and no dessert or bread or anything unhealthy like that.

I feel so good when I do that, and I usually lose weight and look better. But my body must hate being healthy; as soon as I get my weight down, my body comes down with a sniffly cold. Then my body starts telling me, "Feed a cold and starve a fever." Before I realize it, I'm back to a daily dose of fried chicken, burgers, fries, and desserts.

Speak to my body, Lord. Tell it about moderation and a balanced diet. Since it likes old sayings so much, tell it, "The human being does not live by buttered bread alone."

In the face of so many terrible problems in the world, Lord, I know this must sound like an awfully measly one—but it's important to me. I want to teach myself to eat healthy foods and be responsible enough to take good care of this body You've given me to live in.

Help me, Lord. Teach me to take a prayer break instead of a doughnut break. Remind me to take walks instead of second helpings. Help me to sacrifice the sausage-mushroom-pepperoni pizza and have a mushroom-pepper omelet instead. (Say! That sounds good. Maybe if I learn to cook healthy, I can trick my body into thinking it's OK to eat some of that stuff!)

Thank You, Lord, for my body—and please help me to make it shape up!

When I Feel Taken For Granted

IS IT POSSIBLE TO RETURN your family for a refund, Lord? Quick—where is the exchange window? I am ready to trade them in.

I mean, I have had it. I'm not putting up with these people anymore. I am sick of getting walked all over all the time—and I want their feet off my back.

What do they think I am—a garbage truck? They keep dumping on me all the time: all their leftover troubles and complaints and gripes and snipes.

What do they think I am, a mass-transit system? They make elaborate plans to attend every kind of event possible—parades, parties, ball games, bonfires, balloon launches—all scheduled to be held at the farthest reaches of town in uncharted subdivisions and unknown neighborhoods. And, of course, I am the one who is always "volunteered" as the mode of transportation.

What do they think I am, a bank and trust company? Every day it's some new kind of financial plea bargaining. They plead, they bargain, then they expect me to come up with the money and trust they will somehow pay it back.

And that's just the tip of the iceberg, Lord. I could give You lists, I could tell You stories, I could.... Well, You know. Yes, I guess You know all too well—because now that I think about it, those are all the things I do to You. I dump all my troubles on You. I expect You to transport me safely through life, even though I insist on going where *I* want to go—taking strange turns, unsafe alleyways, and unbeaten paths—instead of following where You lead. And I am always pleading and bargaining.

Forgive me, Lord. Help me give my family the kind of patience and gentle understanding You give me.

And, Lord, You know I wouldn't really want to exchange them for any other family in the whole world. But on days like today, it sure would be nice to swap them for a new, improved model just for a couple of hours!

When I'm Lonely

HOW LONG THE DAY, how lonely the night. It isn't easy, Lord, being alone. No one could understand until they lived it awhile.

Mothers with small children often talk about how the walls seem to shake with the noise and how they long for a few quiet moments alone. They don't know what it's like, Lord, when the house is *always* quiet. How wonderful it would be to have just a little laughter, a little conversation, a few moments to share with someone.

And yet I know, Lord, that I am not really alone. You are with me. And *You* know what it is like. You spent forty days and forty nights in the desert. You know what the quiet is like, the hunger, the terrible aloneness.

Help me learn to use my time alone to grow closer to You, to learn more of the mysterious magnificence of Your ways, the beauty of Your plan, the wonders of Your creation. And when I have the opportunity, Lord, help me to reach out to give love and companionship to others, so that they will never have to be as lonely as I have been.

Teach me to use my quiet time to study and discover and pray.

But, Lord, if there are *any* people in this neighborhood who have five minutes to spare in conversation, would you *please* send them to my front door?

When I'm Mad At You, Lord

WHY ME, LORD? Why does everything have to happen to me? Why does everybody else seem to have more happiness and less stress, more love and less hurt, more sweet success and fewer bitter pills to swallow?

They say trials and traumas build courage; difficulties teach you how to cope; and overcoming tragedy gives you strength. But I'm tired, Lord, of being brave and strong and having to cope. I want to rest easy, dream dreams, and just coast for a while. I want to taste the good life and forget about sacrifice and service.

At least, that's what I *thought* I wanted, Lord. Then I started thinking about others; I thought about a young woman whose husband has terminal cancer. I thought about another couple whose four-year-old son just died. I thought about those who live with emotional or physical pain day after day and hour after hour. I thought of those parents who fear for their children's welfare because they live in violent neighborhoods. I thought about those who face financial insecurity with very little to rely on as they face their aging years.

Help me to remember these people, Lord, when I face my small troubles. Help me learn to accept and trust. Forgive my questioning, my whining, my doubting. Teach me to say with love, "Why *not* me?"

Part IV

As My Day Ends...

And I Accomplished Nothing

LORD, YOU KNOW EVERYTHING, so could you please tell me where I can go to get a twenty-five-hour-a-day clock and an eight-day-a-week calendar?

You see, Lord, here I am, at the end of the day, and it looks like I haven't accomplished anything. I've been busy, plugging along steadily since I got out of bed this morning, but can You see anything I've accomplished? Why doesn't my busy-ness ever turn into anything that shows? Why doesn't my work turn into something somebody will notice?

Where is my Eiffel Tower, my symphony, my bridge over troubled waters, my golden spatula sign announcing, "Two Million Burgers Barbecued in Backyard!"?

Maybe my problem is that I want to do everything. I want to read all the books in the library, plant every flower in the seed catalog, visit every country in the world and every doughnut shop in my neighborhood, explore the Internet and outer space—and maybe even join a committee.

So, I guess I answered my own question, Lord. I'm too busy *doing things* to do *anything*.

No wonder I keep going through life a day late and a dollar short. I need help, Lord. Could you please send a bolt of lightning to show me how to turn the countless puzzle pieces of my life into an accomplishment?

Yes, I know—that's not Your job; it's mine. You did Your job when You figured out how to make the world whirl without any of us falling off, when You got the sun to come up and go down every day, when You made all those funny looking animals (especially the ones called "people"). You did Your job—and now it's my turn to figure out how to do mine and fit it into twenty-four-hour days and seven-day weeks.

Lord, thank You for my life. Teach me to not waste a minute of it. Help me to use it to do what You want me to do with it instead of just talking about it and worrying about what to do next. Show me how to live today so that someday I can live with You in eternity—because You and I know, Lord, that timeless eternity is the only place I will ever manage to do all the things on my "to-do" agenda.

And It's Tuna Again

WELL, IT'S TUNA FISH for supper again, Lord—and that means trouble.

According to a trivia tidbit I found, the word *tuna* comes from a Hebrew word meaning "great sea monster." I think my family has been taking Hebrew lessons behind my back because every time I serve tuna, they act as though they are being attacked by a great sea monster. They groan, clutch their throats, and stare at me wide-eyed with a pained expression that says I have betrayed them again. Of course, they act the same way when I serve them okra—and I don't think that comes from Hebrew. I think okra just comes from the South—maybe New Orleans.

But today I don't even know where *I'm* coming from. I'm sick of tuna, too. I would like to groan and clutch my throat and leave for New Orleans or downtown or down the street or even for Hebrew lessons.

I would like to eat supper at any table other than the one in my kitchen—preferably a table with a bouquet of fresh flowers and a linen cloth and a tall goblet of ice water and a silver coffeepot. I would like to have energizing adult conversation served up as an appetizer, and I would like to have a gourmet surprise as an entree—anything other than sea monster with noodles. I also would like some kind words of encouragement and support for dessert.

I know I can't have everything I want, so I guess I'll settle for dinner at the kitchen table again. I'll stick a potted plant in the center of the table, have some "How was your day" conversation, and cover up the sea monster with some shredded cheese.

I'll try to remember that some of Your best friends were fishermen, Lord, so I guess You would approve of our humble meal, even though You probably wouldn't approve of my attitude. Help me, Lord, to do something about that attitude. Help me to accept—and enjoy—what I have. Help me to see the beauty of living my life in the place where You have put me—instead of yearning to be someplace else.

And, Lord, please remind me to put hamburger on my grocery list for tomorrow. (I wonder if that means "great land monster.")

And I'm Sad

I'VE BEEN PLAYING hide-and-seek all day, Lord, and now the day is over and I am sad—very sad.

I've been hiding from reality and seeking help in all the wrong directions. Whenever anything went wrong today, Lord, I hid my eyes or looked away and refused to take responsibility for the moment. I hid from the possibility that any blame could belong to me, pretending that it was all someone else's fault.

And you know what, Lord? I even hid when things went right, as much afraid to take credit as I was to admit fault. Instead of accepting a compliment gracefully, I laughed it off, too unsure of my judgment to even accept the responsibility of praise.

And when I wasn't hiding, I was seeking—looking for reassurance and comfort. I tried to find it in food, entertainment, friends, family, coworkers. I sought but did not find.

What is it with me, Lord? When am I going to stop this endless game of hide-and-seek? You and I both know that the only way I can stop hiding is to face myself—my limitations and my capabilities. I have to start growing toward my potential. I have to take the next step and get on with my life. I have to build on my good points and face my weaknesses. And the only way I can do that is to seek help from the Source of all help—from You, Lord.

I don't want to feel sad at the end of my day, Lord. I want to feel joyful because I have taken Your advice: "Seek, and you will find; knock and it will be opened to you."

And I'm Glad

WELL, HERE IT IS, the end of another day, Lord—and once again, I didn't get treated the way I deserved. Thank goodness.

As usual, I overscheduled and couldn't get everything done. When my husband came home after a busy day at work, I was running around the house like a guillotined chicken, trying frantically to catch up on all the things I hadn't finished yet. Naturally, I was in a bad mood, and, naturally, I took it out on him. But I didn't get what I deserved.

He was kind and sympathetic. He even went out and brought in hamburgers for supper so I wouldn't have to cook.

I should have expected it. It had been like that all day. I had called to complain about a mistake in a bill and was so mad I was really rude to the woman who answered the phone. She, in contrast, was gracious and soft-spoken, quickly handling the problem.

Next, I was racing to a meeting and pulled up at a stop sign. I was in such a hurry that I couldn't stop fast enough to keep from tapping the rear fender of the car in front of me. Luckily, there was no damage, and before I could say anything, the driver was telling me he was sorry for stopping short in front of me.

The meeting lasted longer than I had expected, so I was late getting to school to pick up the kids, and they had gone off to play with their friends on the playground. This meant I had to park the car and go looking for them. Of course, this made me even later, so I was short-tempered and fussing and fuming when we got in the car, complaining about life in general and their muddy shoes in particular. And then my son produced the poster he had made in class—a beautifully crayoned stick figure that was supposed to be me, standing in front of our house. It was lettered, "I love Mommy."

Well, Lord, I am glad this day is over. If anything else had happened, I might have gotten what I deserved.

Thank You, Lord, for letting me squeeze through today. Thank You for all the loving, kind, considerate people in my life who overlook my undeservingness. Please help me to be more like them. Help me to be more prudent, less stressed, and more willing to overlook the shortcomings of others—to do unto them as they have been doing unto me.

And I'm Waiting Up

IT'S MIDNIGHT, LORD. And a few minutes ago I heard some sirens coming from the direction of the highway. The kids should have been home by now. Where are they, Lord?

It's so hard waiting for teenagers, Lord—trying to pretend they're old enough to take care of themselves, while in your heart you still feel you should be holding them by the hand. Help me, Lord. Hold *my* hand.

Remind me of last week, when I was so worried and then they came bouncing in, penitently explaining that they had given someone a ride home and it had been farther and taken longer than they expected. Remind me that You are with them and will watch over them, because I have entrusted them to Your care ever since they were babies. Tell me again—they passed the driving test and got a license, and if the police think they are capable of driving, then I should think so, too.

Yes, I know all those things, Lord, but at midnight mothers don't think with their brains, only with their fast-beating hearts.

What was that, Lord? Was that the sound of a car in the driveway? Yes, it was. And I hear them giggling. They're OK, Lord. They're safe. The wait is over—at least for tonight. Thank You, Lord, thank You.

And I'm Suffering From Noise Overload

LORD, HELP US POOR PARENTS who have music everywhere—in our kitchen and basements, our cars, and our sleep. We taught our children to share, but now they think they have to share their music with us—day and night, upstairs and downstairs, and even out into the traffic! Do you guess that they think music is the glue that keeps a family together?

Whatever they think, we parents think we are on the verge of noise overload. How did we go so fast from lullabies to music that gives mothers pierced ears and fathers terminal temper loss?

Lord, help us. Give us tolerance and understanding and some fail-safe earplugs.

But, Lord, before I go any further, I have to confess something. Last month, my son and I drove to a nearby city to visit some friends, and he took along his favorite CDs. Trapped in a moving vehicle, I was forced to really listen to his music, and I have to confess, Lord, I really liked some of it. Not *all* of it. Not most of it. But *some* of it.

I realized I had been making a generalization again—condemning my son's judgment without giving it a fair trial. We parents are bad about that, Lord. It's so easy to judge in haste and repent at leisure. Help us learn to hesitate—not to be so quick to condemn our teens' friends, clothes, hair, likes and dislikes, *before* we take a second look.

Help us remember, Lord, what it was like when we were young. Nudge us to get out the family album and look at "the way we were." Some of our clothes looked awful, and we chose some friends our parents weren't too sure about, and even some of our music was pretty bad.

So, Lord, help us remember and sympathize and endure. But, Lord, could You please arrange an electrical storm every so often so the power will go out and we can at least have a little peace and quiet in our heads and in our homesteads?

And I'm Lost in Space

IT'S TOO MUCH FOR ME, LORD. I just can't seem to get excited about looking toward a future where I will be taking a space shuttle to visit Aunt Sue, serving a dinner that has been pulverized into baby food and has to be sucked from a tube or maybe even just swallowed like an aspirin, and walking around in a silver-colored spacesuit that has built-in air hoses, oxygen pumps, and a size sixty-four waistline.

Oh, I know, the next generation have their bags all packed to leave for another planet on the first tourist-class ticket they can get. And they think it is all so exciting, challenging, and a chance to get away from the earth where everything is so boring!

Space may be OK for the next generation, but it's a little more complicated for us folks who are used to having our feet on the ground and our hamburgers on the kitchen table.

But today, Lord, I was reading in the encyclopedia about Your bromeliads—the plants that live in trees in Your rain forests. Their roots have no soil, but somehow they survive happily perched on a branch, drinking in the air and sunlight—while the other plant families are busily trying to lead a normal life and find a home for their roots on the good old terra firma.

Do you think I could learn to be bromelieaceous, Lord, and adjust to a new way of living as well as thinking? There's only one problem. The encyclopedia said that in most cases it had taken the bromeliads thousands of years to make the adjustment! I don't have that long, Lord. And some people think our planet doesn't either. We need help.

Remind us, Lord, that our part of the world was discovered by a bunch of people who thought their ship might fall off the edge of the earth at any moment. Help us realize that just a few hundred years ago, people probably thought about America the way we think about space—a new land, unexplored, with unknown terrors and a whole new lifestyle.

Help us poor mortals, not only to accept the inevitability of the future but to welcome it as still another fascinating page in the very slowly unfolding story of Your universe and Your creation. And thank You, Lord, for the unknown and the unexpected. They teach us to put our trust in You.

And I'm Pushing The Panic Button

THIS WEEK WAS FULL of panic and pandemonium, Lord—and just when I should have been praying, I was busy doing everything else.

Why does this always happen? You know I usually check in with You every day. It may just be a short hello instead of a long prayer, but I usually find time to tell You of my woes and worries, and sometimes I even make it to church in the middle of the week instead of waiting until Sunday. And when a friend is in trouble, I pray long and hard, begging for Your help and mercy.

But when I'M the one in trouble, it's a different story. When I push the panic button, I get so involved in working my way out of the current crisis or confusion, I can't seem to slow down long enough to remove myself from the problem far enough to pray.

Last week, when my husband was in the hospital for minor surgery, I was busy dashing back and forth, handling things at home alone, taking him everything he might need before he could notice he needed it, being sure to smile and soothe, comfort and cajole. But I found very little time to pray for him. It wasn't a life-threatening situation, but it was still serious. And I should have been burning up the hot line, begging You to be sure all went well—but I was too busy.

When I get sick myself, Lord, it's the same thing. I am busy

concentrating on how sick I feel and blaming myself for getting sick in the first place and trying to think of anything I could possibly do to get better fast. And every time I try to pray, I just feel too miserable to contact You. Of course, I have never been critically ill. That might be a different story. I would be so scared then that I would probably be crying on Your doorstep day and night.

But it isn't just illness that puts a short circuit in my prayer signals Lord—it's any kind of pandemonium. When I overschedule my week or everything seems to happen at once—when there's a family crisis at home, a busy workload at the office, and a project to be finished for church all at the same time—I never seem to work You into my schedule, too, Lord. Forgive me.

Remind me, Lord, that ten minutes with You, letting Your peace and encouragement wash over me, could give me the strength and confidence to conquer the crisis and calm the confusion.

The next time I push the panic button, Lord, remind me to push the prayer button at the same time.

And I'm Oh So Tired

LORD, MY HUSBAND MAY LOOK YOUNG, but I'm afraid he's nearing his second childhood. You know how small children always speak in words instead of sentences—"Hungry," "Popsicle™," "No!"? Well, my husband has started doing that at dinner. He'll come home from work very tired and sit down to eat, and his table conversation will consist of "Napkin," "Bread," "Potatoes."

When I try to *subtly* tell him, "Dear, the proper phrase is 'Please pass the potatoes,'" he replies, "gravy."

I guess I could put up with that, but what if "the sins of the father are repeated in the son"? What if my son starts saying "Ketchup," "Pickles," "Soda"? Well, at least I know I can occasionally expect to hear at least *two* consecutive words from my son. I know he will say "No carrots" and "No green beans."

Lord, forgive me for being so nitpicky. My husband is so tired some days. I should be grateful he works so hard for us and comes home to dinner every night, instead of expecting him to be as clever and charming as a guest on a talk show. I guess he might appreciate it if I would stop making digs about his etiquette and try to be a bit more clever and charming myself. But I am tired, too, Lord. I have also worked hard all day and battled some frustrations and problems of my own.

So, Lord, please bless both Your tired children. Help us to

comfort each other instead of feeling resentment and trying to vent our hostilities on each other. Help us each to understand the other's irritation. At the end of the long, tiring day, stir our love to share a kiss of peace.

And I Forgot My List

I FORGOT MY LIST this morning, Lord, so I was lost all day—without anything to tell me what to do or where to go next. The list-of-the-day is my compass, my coworker, and sometimes my conscience—"Gotta get it done!"

Is that all life is, Lord? Years and years of making lists—things to pick up or pick out, places to drop in or things to drop off, hurry-ups and forget-me-nots? Is life just a list of chores to complete, meetings to attend, bills to pay?

I may sometimes seem listless, Lord, but I am never list-less.

The worst part is that I usually manage to get most of the dutiful, necessary things crossed off my list eventually (although always later than I expected)—but I seldom get to cross off the unnecessary fun things I'd just *like* to do someday. So I ask You, Lord, when is someday coming?

I'm tired of crossing off things like "get winter clothes out of storage" instead of "buy new swimsuit for trip to Hawaii"; I'm tired of crossing off things like "plan meeting agenda" instead of "plan picnic in the park."

You can see I need help, Lord. Remind me to put *You* at the top of all my lists, and let Your peace soothe my fretting and fuming. Remind me of all the people who are alone and would like to have lists like mine, lists loaded with errands to run and outings to plan and things to do with people they love.

Thank You, Lord, for giving me family and friends who count

on me and share with me and *want* me to be involved in their comings and goings. Help me to better organize my chores and my plans so that at the end of my day, I can look back at those little pockets of time when I was able to do something "just for me."

And thank You, Lord, for keeping me on *Your* list of frenzied friends who are lucky enough to have a life busy enough to need a list to live by.

And I've Got Sand in My Shoe

"IT'S NOT THE MOUNTAIN AHEAD—it's the grain of sand in your shoe."

Now, Lord, that is the story of my life. I look back on today and realize that I weathered a few storms, even some thunderclaps, but when the sun didn't shine on my parade or it started to drizzle on my daydream, I began to self-destruct. I can handle the devastating traumas of my day, but not the irritating trifles. I just can't take life with a grain of sand!

Forgive my impatience, Lord. Teach me how to cope, how to survive the little stresses of the day. Teach me how to smile in spite of the sand in my shoe—or to find a way to get rid of it without complaining and boring everyone else with my troubles.

Help me, Lord. Give me the stick-to-itiveness to work out the trifles of the day—and to learn to shovel out those grains of sand before they turn into sand dunes. And while You're at it, Lord, "Give me patience—but hurry."

And I'm Back Where I Started

STOP THE WORLD—I want to get a transfer!

There must be another planet somewhere where I can get a little rest. I'm tired of this rat-race existence, Lord. "Hurry up and wait" has become a way of life—and I want a way out.

Lord, do You know what it's like to always live on a treadmill—because that's certainly the way I feel here at the end of my day? I feel like those little gerbils who live in cages with exercise wheels—running, running, running, but never getting anywhere except back where they started.

On this planet, Lord, I seem to hurry madly through traffic to get to an appointment on time—and then I sit there only to wait. It might be two minutes or two hours. It might be the doctor, the dentist, the auto-repair shop or the haircut-repair shop. Whatever or wherever it is, everybody thinks their time is more important than mine. I'm expected to be on time, but they are not.

I am tired of playing the waiting game, Lord. I am tired of being hurried and harried, frazzled and frustrated, at every turn, all day long. I'm also tired of polluted air and chemically saturated water, ruthless traffic jams and nasty x-rated everything, politicians' empty promises and taxpayers' empty pockets. This planet is giving me palpitations, pains in the neck, and a plumb pitiful outlook on life. I want a transfer, Lord.

Of course, I know this is the coward's way out. And yes, I have heard it said, "If you can't change the circumstance, change the attitude." And I will admit that my attitude needs attention. I know I should try the power of positive thinking and the mind-over-matter technique, and I should be able to practice self-hypnosis or transactional analysis or go eat a banana split so I will feel better. But will that change the world, Lord? After I make myself feel better, will things actually *be* any better?

Oh, I hear You, Lord. The world is not and never has been perfect. My generation does not have a patent on imperfection. So I should not be so down-mouthed about the current status of the planet. It's been in trouble before, and its people have endured and persevered and survived.

But it *is* maddening, Lord, and I need You to help me to be more than a survivor. Take me off this treadmill so that I don't end my day feeling like I'm right back where I started.

Starting tomorrow, Lord, help me to make a difference. I know I can only change *the* world by changing *my* world, so help me remember that I have to start with myself. Help me to have a more positive attitude, to pray harder, to work harder, to be more patient and more understanding with my fellow travelers.

Help all your people on this planet, Lord, to know what to do and when to do it to change things for the better, so that we can start remaking the world into Your kingdom. And then we won't feel like asking for a transfer.

And I Pay Attention

THIS EVENING, THE HORIZON is wearing evening clothes—a fancy dress suit that is dazzling and dramatic. It's a feast for the eyes—a banquet of orange and tangerine, honey and butter. It's a balm for the soul—garlands of violet and poppy-reds and blue forget-me-nots. Yes, it's sunset time.

Every day it comes and every day it's different. Every day someone, somewhere, stops to revel in the glory. Every day someone, somewhere, is too busy to notice. Today, this evening, this moment, is mine. The glory belongs to me. I watch while the horizon changes and transforms as an Artist's hand mixes in new colors, new shadings, new brilliance. And I have to watch attentively because soon it will be gone, never to be quite the same again. It's always sad to say good-bye but sunset is not sad. Sunset is gloriously full of promise because I know that tomorrow a new day will dawn and the sun will rise again. It always has. It always does. It's one of the few constants left in this unstable universe.

Thank You, Lord, for the sunset promise of tomorrow. Thank You for so many evening blessings—a safe bed to sleep in, a dry roof over my head, a soft pillow, a warm blanket. Thank You for a chance to say I'm sorry for all the mistakes I made today and to give You my own promise to try to do better tomorrow. Thank You for all the second chances You've given me. And for all the sunsets. And now good night.

Part V

I'm Grateful...

For the New

THANK YOU, LORD, for new potatoes and new years; for a new slate, a new page, a new chance; new ideas and newel posts and newspapers with good news.

Thank You for that good-morning feeling of wearing new clothes, and for the surprises I get when I see the world anew through the eyes of a small child.

New is wonderful, Lord. It's the dawn coming up like thunder, the first cry of a newborn baby, the first step, the first tooth, the first dance, the first victory. New is the world forever being renewed. Thank You, Lord, for all the newness in a very old world.

Thank You, Lord, for continually showing me that You did not create the world a very long time ago but are still creating it today, forever renewing it and unfolding it to me.

And thank You, Lord, for the promise—for the assurance that as wonderful as this world is, it is just a tiny part of Your universe, just a tiny taste of the endless newness waiting to be discovered in eternity.

For the Old

THANK YOU, LORD, for old shoes and old friends; old cheese and old customs; lovely old books and exquisite antiques. I love them all.

Thank You for old jokes and old snapshots and old memories; old clothes that make me feel good when I wear them; old dogs that really do learn new tricks.

Thank You for old family traditions, old boots that keep out the snow, and old recipes that never fail.

It's funny, Lord, how we like to go through old trunks and old scrapbooks and relive old times, but we don't much like to visit old people or have them around us. There was a time, Lord, when everything old was venerated and honored—especially old people. It isn't that way anymore. But it should be.

Help me, Lord, to see that in age there is beauty and wisdom and grace. Teach me to better appreciate our ancestors and our heritage and to give them honor and attention and respect.

Thank You, Lord, for the older generation—for my roots, my bedrock, my foundation. Teach me—teach us all—to love and cherish old people as much as we cherish old mementos.

For the Blues

I'VE GOT THE BLUES TODAY, LORD. Thank You.

Thank You for the blue of today's sky! Thank You for the blue-bird that appeared out of the blue this morning to show off his feathers and stuff himself at the bird feeder. Thank You for the bluebells in bloom along the path, and for the blueberries for breakfast. I can see this is going to be a blue day!

Thank You for the wonderful surprises that are more special because they show up only once in a blue moon. Thank You for bluegrass music and the blues in the night that pass as soon as the blue sky of morning appears. Thank You for the special blue-print for my life that filled my days with beautiful music and only a few blue notes to make the others even sweeter.

Thank You for the blues, Lord, and the pinks and the purples and the oranges and the yellows and the greens. How wonderful that You chose to fill our world with color, Lord. It wouldn't have been the same if it had all been color-less. It wouldn't have been the same if we had never known what it's like to have the blues!

For the Bolds

WHAT WOULD WE DO without them, Lord—the bold campaigners who fight for truth and justice; the bold adventurers who thrill us and inspire us with their bold deeds; the bold believers who spread Your word wherever they go.

Bold is beautiful, Lord. We can't all achieve it, but we stand in awe of those who can live their lives in a style as bold and bright as a brass band marching down Main Street.

Thank You, Lord, for the bold proclaimers throughout history who courageously took a stand; for the bold explorers who widened the globe; for the bold researchers who discovered medical cures or a new star or a new toothpaste; for the bold apostles who brought the world a New Testament.

Thank You, too, Lord, for the bolds in nature; the dramatic thunderstorms and crashing ocean waves; the flamingos and the orchids and the volcanoes. They get our attention and remind us of Your power and majesty.

Thank You, Lord, for all the bolds. They are the exclamation points that change the *ooohs* in our lives to OOOHS!

For So Many Splendid Things

THANK YOU, LORD, for so many splendid things—
For fireworks and violets and hummingbird wings;
For a warm, cozy room on a cold, blowy day;
For friends who always know just the right things to say;
For the giggles and wiggles of a class of first-graders;
For the tooth-missing grins of small baseball-card traders;
For cookies—both the fortune and the chocolate chip;
For our bags all packed for that vacation trip;
For those inventive, creative, idealistic teen dreamers;
For birthday parties, balloons, and crepe-paper streamers;
For morning and evening and the sunshine of noon;
For faith and hope and the promise of "soon."

Thanks Lord, for the fascination of a world ever new,
since its mystery and beauty are reflections of You.

For All the Seasons

THANKS
for the enthusiasms of springtime:
the plans for huge vegetable gardens
and ambitious summer travels
and swim parties and cookouts
and lazy sunny afternoons
to spend with a book and a tall glass of lemonade;
for the promise of something wonderful to come,
evidenced by the appearance of tender green buds
on cold, hard, bare branches;
for the spring in my step
and the spring fever in my head and heart,
for crocus and forsythia and buttercups and Easter.

THANKS
for the honeyed warmth of summertime:
for the giggles of little girls
running through the water sprinkler;
butterflies and fireflies on the wing;
the sound of the cricket in the twilight;
the earthy, rich deliciousness of homegrown ripe tomatoes;
the one-of-a-kind liquid/solid sensation

of cold watermelon on the tongue;

the surprise of a sudden summer shower,

cutting through the stillness

with its pitter-patter on the roof,

cutting through the heat to bring a gentle, cooling breeze.

THANKS

for the harvesttime richness of autumn:

for the multicolored Halloween costumes

worn by the trees;

for the pumpkin on the vine and in the pie;

for the surprise of a warm sunny afternoon

when a cold drizzle had been predicted;

for trick-or-treat time and bonfires

and roasted hot dogs and toasted marshmallows

and Thanksgiving Day.

THANKS

for the holiday expectation of winter:

for the excitement of shopping trips

and finding just the right gift for someone special;

for the rustle and crinkle of gift-wrapping paper,

for the secrets hiding behind the shimmer

of satin ribbons and bows;

for snowball fights and snowflakes on the windowpane;

for clear, crisp mornings and warm fireside visits;
for Advent prayers and Advent candles;
for the waiting and the watching and the wonder;
and for the "coming" of Christmas.

THANKS, Lord,
for all seasons.